The Colours of Life

SPECKTRUM ART

SPECKTRUM ART

SPECKTRUM ART

ISBN: 978-1-7780059-3-0

SPECKTRUM ART

DEDICATION

For you. For me.
For anyone who may need it.

This poetry collection is written for people who have suffered/are suffering from depression, anxiety, any and all struggles with mental health and those going through a difficult time in their lives.

Creating art and writing has always helped me with my journey to mental wellness. I hope this collection will be able to help you in some way even if it's just a little.

2

ACKNOWLEDGMENTS

Thank you to my incredible wife for always being my number one fan, encouraging me and believing in my dreams.

Thank you to family and friends who have always supported me.

Thank you to all who chose to follow my journey with art and poetry.

SPECKTRUM ART

SECTIONS

The complete opposite of my first poetry
collection, this book is not divided into
chapters. I wrote the poems as they came
along through the thoughts, feelings and
experiences that evoked them.

Feel free to read in the order you prefer!

Sit back, get cozy and don't be afraid to feel
what needs to be felt.

...

THE COLOURS OF LIFE

...

SPECKTRUM ART

A simple smile from a stranger
Could be enough
To keep someone out of danger
From themselves

Life gave me you
So I'm giving you my life
Every single day
All that I am
Forever yours

Perfection is an illusion
that can never be attained.
It's time to rearrange your aim.

The best remedy I have found
To chase away the dark clouds
Is to wrap myself in your arms
Listening to the beat of your heart

<u>Twin Flame</u>

Maybe, just maybe
We are all meant to be broken
In some way or form
Maybe, just maybe
We are meant to find the one
That helps us pick up the pieces off the floor
Maybe, just maybe
Both of you put together make a whole
Maybe, just maybe
This is the twin flame of your soul

Don't believe me?
Well then just watch me grow.
Into a stronger, wiser, kinder
person than I was before.

Use your strength to fight for good
and to defend those who are weak.

Flirting With Death

Those days
Where you just want to push
The gas pedal past the brake

Close your eyes
Take a deep breath
And feel your heart race

Let go of the steering wheel
Leave it up to fate
To decide if it's your time to go or stay

Unbuckle your seat belt
So you can concentrate on something
Other than the way you felt

Those days
When you are flirting with death
Just to see what you will get

Too Much

Too much weight on my shoulders
And not enough strength to keep going
My heart is still beating
But it's begging for me to lighten the load

Too much caffeine
And not enough sleep
Thoughts on my mind running wild
But I can barely stand on my feet

Too much silence
And not enough time
To deal with all the demons inside me
But I'm still somehow getting by

I asked you why
Would you want to be with me
When you could be
With someone better
You said
You loved me
Exactly how I am
And that you weren't perfect either

Be kind
But don't let others take advantage of you
Be patient
But don't wait too long
Be strong
But don't be cruel
Be wise
But don't let it overpower you

Smiles are what you see
Deterioration is what I feel
So don't you dare tell me
That my pain isn't real

Those of us
That wear our hearts
On our sleeves
Know what it's like
Having to pick up the pieces
Over and over again
Just hoping it will finally mend
We give until it hurts
Always putting others first
There is something about
Helping others
That helps us
In some way
Just don't forget
To put yourself
First some days

You are enough.
You are beautiful.
You are loved.
Your worth is immeasurable by words.
You have a purpose on this earth.
Today may seem dark,
But tomorrow will be better.
You are not alone,
We are in this together.

Some days
I'm just sitting there
Stuck in a gaze
Trapped in my mind
Depression is the prison
Anxiety the prisoner by my side
The key may be right in front of me
But my eyes are blindfolded
And my hands are tied
I can't see it
I can't reach it
It's unfair to say I haven't tried

The world is burning
The world is melting
We need to make changes
We need to do something

Turning the page
Is easier to say
Than it is to do

Sometimes it feels like
All the pages
Are stuck together with glue

Take the time
That you need
One day you'll be able to

Mental Illness

Mental illness
Isn't just a war we can win
It's a series of battles
We need to fight again and again

Mental illness
Isn't just something we can conquer
And put a trophy on the shelf
It's constantly facing our personal hell

Mental illness
Can affect absolutely anyone
It doesn't matter who you are
Or where you are from

Mental illness
Doesn't define who we are
It's a part of our journey
Proof we have gotten so far

Instead of keeping quiet
I chose to write it
To write it all
Every victory and every fall
What kept me going
And all the times I wanted to stop

Write it all
Until you run out of words
Write it all
Until you no longer feel hurt
Write it all
Until your fingers are sore
Write it all
Until you feel lighter than before
Write it all
Right now to help yourself
Write it all
One day it may help someone else
Write it all

There are so many of us
That have suffered way too much
But I believe that
We are as strong
As all that we have suffered
We are warriors
We are survivors
We are heroes
We are fighters

They tell you "sink or swim"
But I'm telling you
You can learn to adapt
To the environment you're in

People seem to think
It's a magical kind of thing
All of a sudden
Your mental illness disappears
Like it was never really here
But, that's not how it works
You need to be willing
To put in the work
For it to get better
But it's still here

Some Days

Some days my heart is so heavy
It's impossible to carry the weight in my chest
I find it harder not knowing why
It's not like my veins are filled with cement

Some days I just can't fall asleep
Because of the thoughts inside my head
When morning comes it's so hard
I can't find the strength to get out of bed

Some days I can't find any motivation
Even though the sun is out
And the sky is blue
I just can't get out of the house

Some days feel like the worst days
I remind myself that those days
Won't be all of my days
And that I will be okay

I'll help you fight your demons
And I know you'll help fight mine
As long as we are in this together
We will be just fine

It may be selfish
But if I had to choose
Between you and the world
I would choose you
Because you are my world

You're on top of the mountain
You made it
Be proud of what you accomplished
Embrace it

The world is filled with all kinds of people
Some are good, some are bad
And some are purely evil

<u>E.</u>

I still can't believe it
This world
You chose to leave it
Behind
In your honor
I will do my best
To help others
Find their light

If I could have any powers
It would be to help
Help anyone in need
To help those
Who have no roof over their heads
Or nothing to eat
To help those
Who are abused and mistreated
To help those
Whose mental health
Has them feeling defeated

I wish I could save you
I wish I could save me
I wish I could save the world
But I'm just a human being

Deepest Darkest Place

In the deepest
Darkest place in my heart
Hides the demons
That have always been there
From the start

In the deepest
Darkest place in my mind
Lingers the voices
That whisper things
That are unkind

In the deepest
Darkest place in my soul
There's a void
That makes me feel
Like I am not whole

There is no such thing as traditional
When it comes to love
Each love is as unique
As every one of us

Five years ago you stole my heart
So now I'll be taking your name
We will stick together
Through the sunshine and the rain

Forever is a long time
But I'm looking forward to spending it with you
We're counting down the days
Until we say "I do"

You are strong
When I feel weak
When I fall
You help me back on my feet

I am finally at a good place
With my mental health
Some days are good, some are bad
And some feel like hell
But I can finally say that generally
I am doing very well

Home is where the heart is
And my heart is forever yours
No matter where we are
You always make me feel at home

Depression is like the ocean
One day it's calm
And the next is a tsunami
You're just trying to hold on
To whatever you can
Because it feels like you're drowning

You're as warm as the sun
You're as beautiful as a flower
I love you more and more
Every second, minute and hour

Why can't we all
Just help each other grow
Help each other heal

Two lovers
Forever
Two hearts
Beat together
Two souls
Me and you
Two words
I do

I traded my blades
For colored pencils and paint brushes
I stopped adding scars
And started creating art
Drawings, Paintings, Poetry
All helped me to save me

Healing takes time.
You need to be patient.

The day that we met
I was as nervous as it gets
Never mind butterflies in my stomach
I had the animal kingdom in my chest
I remember it like it was yesterday
The look in your eyes
Smile on your face
Little did I know
That it was the beginning
Of the rest of our days

The kind of words you don't want to hear
From someone you endear:

"I have leukemia… you know what that is?"

The ring on my finger
To this day
Still makes me shiver
How grateful I am to be hers
Those two words
Have changed my world

What does forever look like?

She has brown eyes
Somewhere in between
Golden honey and milk chocolate
Depending on the light

She has a smile
That makes my heart
Skip a beat
Every single time

She has a soul
So pure
I'm not even sure
How I got to be hers

She has arms that are magic
A safe haven
For all the days
That I don't feel okay

What does forever look like?

It looks like her.

Depression and anxiety
I will carry them with me
For the rest of my life
Some days they are heavy
Some days they are light

Mental illness is a life sentence
Without any chances of parole
There's no bail you can pay
To make those demons leave you alone

Hurt.
Everybody hurts.
There is no way to measure
who has it better
and who has it worst.

The truth is some days
You'll be winning
And some days you'll be losing
Never give up
Even if it feels like
The finish line is moving
And you're standing still

Do you wish
You could just grab
An eraser, a pen or paintbrush
To fix all the things about yourself
That you don't love

Some days you wake up
It feels like the world
Will stop spinning
And the sun won't rise
When there's more darkness around you
Than when you close your eyes

Relationships are a two way street
Not just one
Some people have the audacity
To complain that I don't visit enough
I don't text, call or drop by
That doesn't mean I don't miss them
And they aren't on my mind

Hold me tight, kiss me goodnight.
Make love to me like it's our last time.

All the stars in the sky
So beautiful as they shine
But nothing compared to
The beauty in your eyes

Look at a cardboard box
At all the weight it can handle
But leave it in the rain
And it will surely dismantle
I believe that as humans
We were born to be both strong and fragile

You are better than you were
I am better than I was
Together we have forged
An indestructible kind of love

I love the look in your eyes
When I tease you
The frustration as I take my time
To please you

I have grown
And I am not the toxic person I was before
Toxic, not as in a bad person
But someone in a bad place
I was just trying to figure out who I was
In a world filled with hate

Age is just a number
Wisdom comes at a cost
It comes down to
What's in your soul
And what's in your heart

Words are just words
But how is it that you can feel them
Louder than they can be heard

We just got a brand new bed
King size, as comfy as a cloud
Yet some days I have trouble sleeping
Because the demons are just too loud
I've been more careful
Making sure I am eating healthy foods
Yet it seems even all those things
Don't even help with my mood

You are my heart
When I feel empty
You are the light
When I can't see clearly
You are the arms
That holds me tightly
You are the warmth
That feels like safety
You are my strength
When I can barely stand on my feet
You are my soul
The one that completes me
You are all that I want and need
You are everything to me

Please know that
If you need to talk to someone
Or if help is taking too long to arrive
Please know I will be by your side

Take a pen and paper
And write
Write until you feel numbness
On the tip of your fingers
Write until your mind
Is clear from danger
Write until all the ink
In your pen has depleted
Write until your heart
Sings the melody of healing
Write until
The page is full
Write until
Your soul is at home

I love when the sun sets
And kisses the horizon

<u>Seasons</u>

Fall is full of strength and vulnerability
Even though the trees leaves fall down
Their roots are firmly planted in the ground

Winter is harsh but so truthful
It brings storms and blistering colds
Yet it is so light and peaceful

Spring is nature's phoenix
Everything blooms stronger and more beautiful
Can you feel it

Summer is full of warmth and happiness
The ocean, the trees, flowers and bees
You can see it all unravelling

Don't be afraid of the dark
You own the moon and all of its stars

You are stronger than your demons.

No matter how impossible it may seem
Even the flowers can grow
Through the cracks of concrete

I will be the voice
For those who can't or won't speak
I am the proof that
Those demons can be beat

My mind is messy
But my heart is pure
I am not perfect
But I am forever yours

I can still feel the scars
Inside of my mouth
That's where it all started
Not wanting anyone to find out
When the pain grew stronger
I cared less and less
Now I have scars
All over
From my toes
To my head

With you I feel safe
Your arms are the barrier
That my demons can't break

I've fallen so many times
That I lost count
I get back up again
Because I don't back down

Sometimes I just want to cry
But I couldn't tell you why
I have no explanations
For the things I can't control

I put work
Before my family
Growing up
It's what they thought me
Working hard
Would make me happy
Success and a good job
Is what they wished for me
Now I have two jobs
And chase my dreams on the side
I'm always busy
Barely have any free time
When I do I take some for me
And spend the rest with my wife

My depression and anxiety
Have been a part of me for so long
They call me home

My demons may stay with me forever
But this is my kingdom
I promise, I will always own them

Living life sober
Is much more difficult
Like a rose, it has thorns
But it is so much more beautiful

The good days
Make the bad days
Worth it
No matter how horrible they are
The depression and anxiety
May never let go of me
But that's okay
Because I'm stronger than they are

I get emotional when I write
My heart is pounding in my chest
And I feel tears in my eyes

Life is like a rose
You work hard for it to bloom
For it to grow
Roses are beautiful
But they can hurt you
If you get pricked
You don't throw it away do you
It is painful but you will heal
And love the rose evermore deeply

Sometimes there's a reason behind it
But often times there is not
There isn't always an explanation
For mental illness

Look at diseases
You can eat well and stay fit
That doesn't make you immune
To getting sick

Who knows
It may be in our genetics or surroundings
But what's important
Is what we do about it

Oh, those brown eyes
When they look at me from bellow
My hands search for something to hold on to
I can't help curling my toes

Homeless

Here I am in a hotel
With 71 out of 74 rooms vacant
But there's nothing I can do
If I was a millionaire
or didn't need this second job
I would have given him a room

Did you know that a lotus
Thrives in an environment
That most flowers would die in
When things get hard
And you feel like you're drowning
Remember, you are a lotus
Not only will you survive
You will bloom
More beautiful than ever

Let's normalize mental health
Let's normalize talking about how we feel
Let's normalize not always being ok
Let's normalize asking for help
Let's normalize a better health care system
Let's normalize a more informed society

I remember feeling so lucky
Having you right next door
No more than a few steps away
That's for sure

I remember afternoons spent
Watching cartoons
Even the silly ones
Such as sailor moon

I remember you waiting in the cafeteria
Where you worked in my grade school
Always with a snack and a smile
It always made my day to see you

I remember you cheering for me
On the benches by the soccer field
I was never the best
But in me you always believed

I remember the family vacations
We spent in Florida and Disney
Those wonderful memories
I will always keep with me

I remember all the wisdom
And guidance you shared with us
All the patience, kindness
Your heart always full of love

I remember
I'll remember always

I used to hear people say
You need to love yourself
Before loving someone else
But I found this to be untrue
Because no one could ever love me
The way you do
I have learned from the best
And now I love me too
We share a kind of love
That is only seen in the movies
The kind most would say is a myth
The only arguments we seem to have
Are about telling the other
Not to touch the dirty dishes
You have proven to me
True love really does exist
My favorite love story
Will always be our very own
You are mine and I am yours
The twin flame of my soul
You complete me and make me better
Together we are one
You and I are forever

Wisdom
In the form
Of carefully
Crafted words
To make you feel

When I look in the mirror
I see my mother
I see my father
I see all the sacrifices they made
For both of their daughters

I am a night owl
I get creative
When people put their lights out
The words pour out of me
Like rain from a dark cloud
When I'm done
The sun is rising
And everything is alright now

You are a thief
You stole my heart
And all of its beats
You took the emptiness
And made me complete

My demons taunt me
Every time I take these pills
Because they were the ones I swallowed
Trying to escape them

I want to be raw
I want to be open
I want to be the person
That I needed when I felt broken

My heart is an inkwell
My feelings the ink
I am the quill-feather
I write it all down
Until I am feeling better

You should see the smile on her face
When we talk about the family
We're going to create

I truly believe magic exists
I can feel it on your fingertips
I can taste it on your lips
Magic

The colours of life

More than just sunshine
There's also the rain
Life is full of happiness
But also some pain
There is the darkness
And there is the light
Everything in between
The colours of life

Dear Reader,

Thank you for taking the time to read this book!

I am no Picasso or Shakespeare, but I have enjoyed creating art for as long as I can remember and am proud of what I create. My intention is to share this collection with the world so that it can hopefully help someone, somewhere out there.

Sincerely,

-K.

ABOUT THE AUTHOR/ARTIST

I grew up in the wonderful small town of Cap-Pele, NB, Canada. I am currently living in another beautiful small town of Bathurst, NB, Canada. I enjoy a little bit of everything in life. I love art in all of its forms (poetry, drawing, painting…). I enjoy gaming out, watching movies and reading. I also enjoy hiking, camping and kayaking. I love cooking and food even more. I am a big fan of tattoos. I enjoy spending time with family and friends when I can. I love my fur babies. Most of all I love my wife, my other half, with all my heart!

-K.

<u>Books by Specktrum Art</u>

From Darkness To Light (poetry)

The Colours Of Life (poetry)

...

Follow my journey through art and poetry!

www.specktrumart.com

 specktrum.art@gmail.com

 SpecKtrum Art

 specktrum.art

SpecktrumA

SPECKTRUM ART

SPECKTRUM ART

SPECKTRUM ART

www.ingramcontent.com/pod-product-compliance
Lightning Source LLC
Chambersburg PA
CBHW032121050726
47591CB00011B/1911